© 2008 White Star S.p.A.
Via Candido Sassone, 22/24
13100 Vercelli, Italia
www.whitestar.it

TRANSLATION: MARCO VISENTIN

ISBN 978-88-544-0402-1

REPRINTS:
1 2 3 4 5 6   12 11 10 09 08

Color separation: Fotomec, Turin
Printed in Thailand

We wish you a

merry
Christmas

WHITE STAR PUBLISHERS

Merry...

Christmas

Merry Christmas

 }

edited by Valeria Manferto De Fabianis

graphic design by Clara Zanotti

Memories . . . . . . of Christmas

Ornaments and . . . decorations

Sweet . . . . . . Christmas

Christmas at the movies

Christmas . . . . . . with four paws

Memories . . .

. . . OF CHRISTMAS

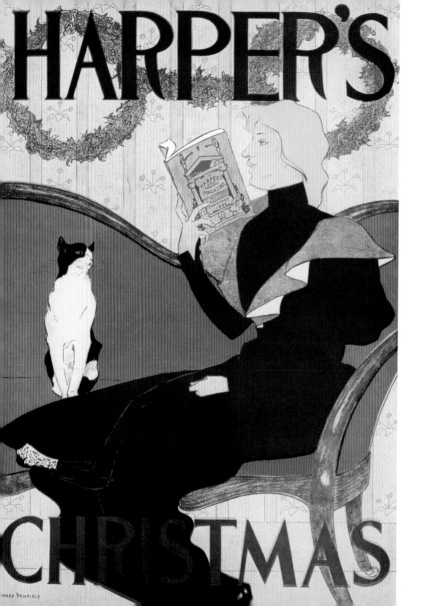

Christmas poster by Edward Penfield for *Harper's Magazine* { 1894 }

Christmas poster by Steve Collier { 2003 }

If you don't have
Christmas
in your heart,
you won't find it
under the tree.

- Cover of Delineator (December 1931) -

DECEMBER 1931

10 CENTS

DELINEATOR

KATHLEEN NORRIS   CONINGSBY DAWSON   LADY ELEANOR SMITH

"Remember this December, that love weighs more than gold."

- Josephine Dodge Daskam Bacon -

{ Cover of *Harper's Bazaar* (December 1931) }

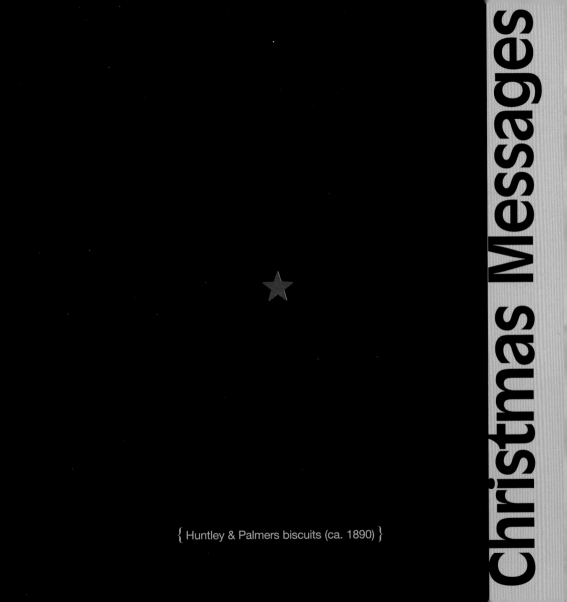

Christmas Messages

{ Huntley & Palmers biscuits (ca. 1890) }

"National
Lottery for
National Aid.
Christmas
1942 draw."

I'M
DREAMING
OF A WHITE
CHRISTMAS

- Bing Crosby, 1942 -

{ Dewar's Whisky (1933) }

{ Martini (1938) }

Coca-Cola { 1952 }

Panettone *Motta* { Milan, 1931 }

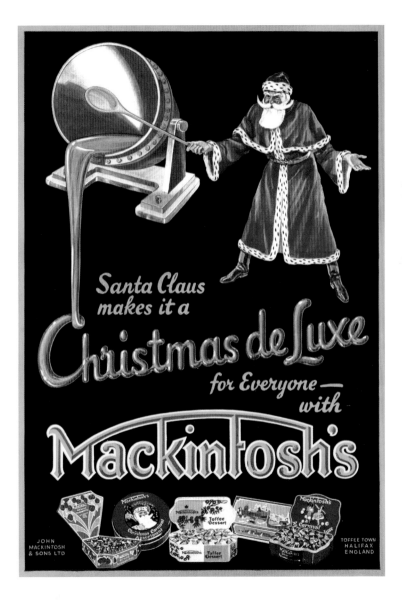

HAPPY
CHRISTMAS
WAR IS
OVER

- John Lennon, 1971 -

German propaganda card

{ Christmas 1915 }

Christmas card

{ late 19th century }

"There is only one Christmas, the rest are just anniversaries"

- James Cameron -

"At Christmas, all roads lead home"

- Marjorie Holmes -

Christmas greetings card { 1916 }

"DEAR SANTA CLAUS, THE PRESENT I WANT THIS YEAR IS . . ."

Christmas card by F.G. Lewin

{1922 }

MERRY CHRISTMAS

{ Greetings card (ca. 1910) }

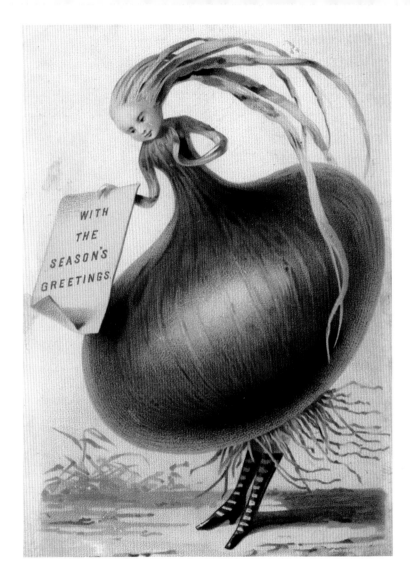

All good things and Best Wishes

Coming!

Christmas Hours so rich in pleasures
Shed on you a royal shower,
And the New Year bring you treasures
Which shall brighten every hour

Here comes the pudding!

{ ca. 1920 }

Christmas pudding

{ ca. 1915 }

Mr. Pudding on a bicycle { 1913 }

Mr. Pudding is worried { ca. 1905 }

Christmas

is already
in the air.

{ United Kingdom, 1910 }

ACCEPT
MY   O
CHRISTMAS
WISHES ⊙

MERRY CHRISTMAS

NOW TELL ME LITTLE ONES WHAT SHALL I BRING, AND I'LL TRY
TO REMEMBER EVERY LITTLE THING, BUT ANYWAY WHETHER OR
NOT, I KNOW IF YOU ARE GOOD YOU'LL GET A WHOLE LOT

{ United Kingdom, ca. 1900 }

{ United Kingdom, ca. 1890 }

WAKE UP !
SANTA
CLAUS
IS HERE.

Drawn by A. C. PECK

"I'LL SAY IT'S TRUE"

Ornaments and . . .

DECORATIONS

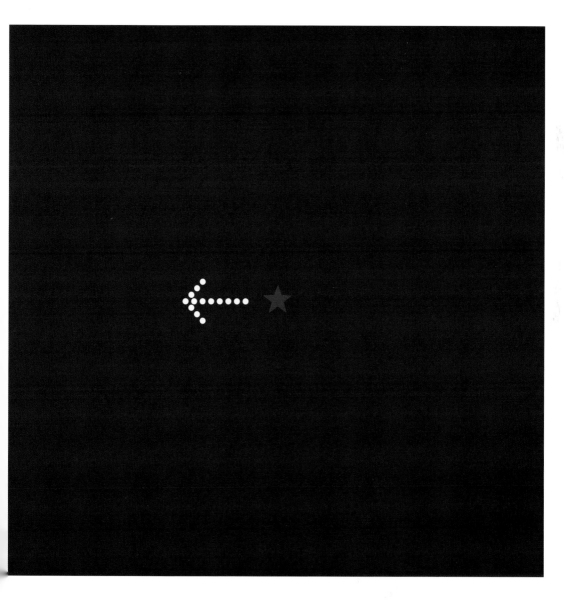

Even the simplest tree holds the magic of Christmas.

YES,
t h i s
Christmas
I will make
a large tree
but instead of
d e c o r a t i o n s ,
I will hang the pictures
of my best friends.

The secret of a great Christmas? Flowers, pinecones ... and a lot of imagination!

Christmas is . . .

...is upon us!

The poor little girl lit a third match
and instantly found herself sitting
under a magnificent
Christmas tree.

**A thousand little candles
were shining and colorful images
danced around the fir tree.**

(Hans Christian Andersen)

And yet there
must be some
logical way to
explain this
thing called
Christmas.

- *from* Nightmare
before Christmas -

Never fear . . . Christmas brings out the best in us!

When Christmas comes . . .

... it comes
to the heart.

Christmas is
not a time of year ...

...it's a state
of mind.

Santa Claus

Santa Claus
comes at night,
he comes
in silence
at midnight.

Santa Claus comes through the snow
... bringing presents to and fro.

Snow falls,
snow falls

Snow falls,
and all is in tumult.

- Snow falls, *Boris Pasternak* -

❄

Sweet . . .

. . . CHRISTMAS

TO DINE AT
HOME ON
THE DAY OF
CHRISTMAS
VIGIL, WHILE
THE QUARTIER
LATIN
EMBELLISHES
ITS WAYS WITH
DAINTY FOOD
AND TEMPTING
RELISHES ?

- La Bohème, *Giacomo Puccini* -

❄

Milk, eggs, sugar . . .

**The ingredients
for a good Christmas.**

CHRISTMAS MUST BE FULLY SAVORED . . .

The sweeter side of Christmas.

What fun it is to ride . . .

. . . in a one-horse open sleigh.

- Jingle Bells, 1857 -

Advent: an anticipation to savor
day by day

Christmas

AT THE MOVIES

Mickey's Christmas song

{ Walt Disney, 1983 }

Mickey's Christmas song

{ Walt Disney, 1983 }

His New Mamma { 1924 }

Christmas scene from a 1920s movie

"OH, DARLING,
WHERE DID
YOU PUT
THE DOG ★
BISCUITS ?
YOU KNOW,
THE BOX
AUNT SARAH
SENT FOR
CHRISTMAS."

Lady and the Tramp

{ Walt Disney, 1955 }

"Once upon
a time - of all
the good days
in the year,
on Christmas Eve -
old Scrooge sat
busy in his
counting-house."

- A Christmas Carol, *Charles Dickens* -

A Christmas Carol

{ Metro-Goldwyn-Mayer, 1938 }

"I've got a Christmas present for you."

"A Christmas gift in the middle of July??"
"Well, we always do our Christmas
shopping early!"

Oliver Hardy and Stan Laurel with presents
{ 1930 }

The Facts of Life { Melvin Frank, 1960 }

Robin and the Seven Hoods { Gordon Douglas, 1964 }

All I Want for Christmas { Robert Lieberman, 1991 }

Bright Eyes { David Butler, 1934 }

Elf { John Favreau, 2003 }

Jingle All the Way { Brian Levant, 1996 }

Mail your
packages early
so the Post Office
can lose them
in time for
Christmas !

- Johnny Carson -

South Park

{ Woodland Critter Christmas, 1997 }

Gonzo started
to narrate:
"It was the
afternoon
of Christmas
Eve and
Scrooge..."

The Muppet Christmas Carol

{ Brian Henson, 1992 }

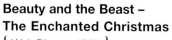

"No one can forbid Christmas"

**Beauty and the Beast –
The Enchanted Christmas**
{ Walt Disney, 1997 }

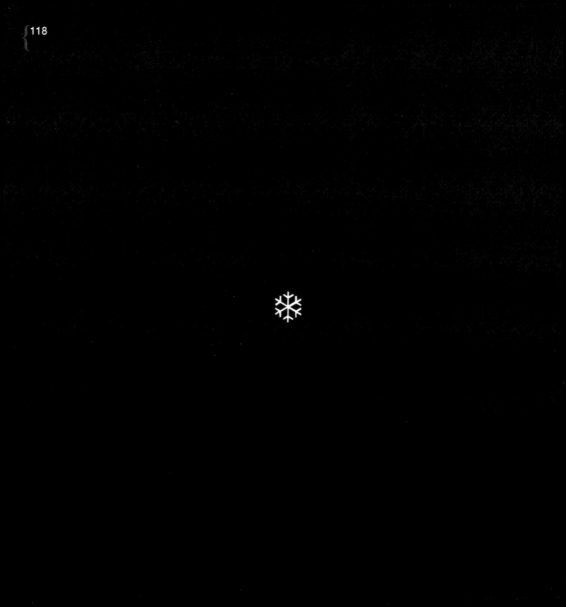

The Grinch { Ron Howard, 2000 }

Polar Express { Robert Zemeckis, 2004 }

NOW,
YOU'VE
PROBABLY
WONDERED
WHERE
HOLIDAYS
COME
FROM.
IF YOU
HAVEN'T,
I'D SAY IT'S
TIME YOU
BEGUN.

Nightmare before Christmas { Tim Burton, 1993 }

Christmas . . .

...WITH FOUR PAWS

Christmas Eve. ❄
❄
❄

Christmas Eve in harmony,
Christmas Day in happiness.

Waiting for . . .

... Santa Claus

Christmas with a surprise

"Kissing under the mistletoe brings good luck."

Small **Medium** **Large ...**

photographic credits

Page 8 The Bridgeman Art Library/Archivi Alinari,Firenze (Father Christmas, 1959 ©Succession Picasso, by SIAE 2008) **Page 12** Swim Ink 2, LLC/Corbis **Page 13** Steve Collier; Collier Studio/Corbis **Pages 15, 17, 18**, Mary Evans Picture Library **Page 21** Roger-Viollet/Archivi Alinari, Firenze **Pages 22, 23** Mary Evans Picture Library **Page 24** Photoservice Electa/AKG Images **Page 26** Archivio Motta-Alemagna, Milano **Page 27** Mary Evans Picture Library **Pages 28, 29, 31** Photoservice Electa/AKG Images **Pages 32, 35** Mary Evans Picture Library **Page 37** Mary Evans Picture Library/Alamy Images **Pages 38, 39, 40, 41, 42, 43** Mary Evans Picture Library **Page 45** Heritage Image Partnership/Olycom **Pages 46, 47, 49** Mary Evans Picture Library **Page 52** Reimar Gaertner/Granata Images **Page 54** Tom Hopkins/ Getty Images **Page 56** Granata Images **Page 58** Bloemenburo Holland/Agefotostock/Marka **Pages 59, 60, 61** Granata Images **Pages 62, 64, 66, 67, 68, 69, 71, 73, 74** Franco Pizzochero/Agefotostock/Marka **Pages 78, 79** Olycom **Page 81** Lawrence Manning/Corbis **Page 83** Shannon O'Hara/Getty Images **Page 85** Olycom **Page 87** Huber-Starke/Masterfile/Sie **Page 88** Bringard Denis/Tips Images **Page 89** Olycom **Page 91** Rosenfeld/Granata Images   **Page 93** Premium/Agefotostock/Marka **Page 96** Walt Disney Co./courtesy Everett / Everett Collection/Contrasto **Page 97** Courtesy Everett Collection/Contrasto **Pages 98, 99** Bettmann/Corbis **Page 101** Courtesy Everett Collection/Contrasto **Pages 102-103** MGM/The Kobal collection **Page 104** John Springer Collection/Corbis   **Page 106** Warner Bros/The Kobal Collection **Page 107** Courtesy Everett Collection/Everett Collection/Contrasto **Page 108** Paramoun/The Kobal Collection **Page 110** 20thCentFox/Courtesy Everett Collection/Contrasto **Page 111** New Line Cinema/Courtesy Everett Collection/Contrasto **Page 113** Comedy Central/Courtesy Everett Collection/Contrasto **Pages 114-115** Rue des Archives **Pages 116-117** Buena Vista Pictures/Courtesy Everett Collection/Contrasto **Page 119** Imagineent/Batzdorff,Ron/The Kobal Collection **Pages 120-121** Castle Rock/Shangri-La Entertainment/The Kobal Collection **Page 123** Buena Vista Pictures/Courtesy Everett Collection/Contrasto **Pages 126, 127, 129, 130, 131, 132, 133** Jane Burton/Warren Photographic **Page 134** Alison Barnes Martin/Masterfile/Sie **Pages 136-137** Mark Taylor/Warren Photographic **Pages 139, 140, 141** Jane Burton/Warren Photographic **Page 143** Courtesy Everett Collection/Contrasto